The Hundredth Hour

poems of new mamahood

by

Kitt Healy

Finishing Line Press
Georgetown, Kentucky

The Hundredth Hour

poems of new mamahood

ACKNOWLEDGMENTS

Many thanks to all who reviewed these poems and encouraged me to finally
do something with them. This includes: Anders Gurda, Kjerstin Gurda, John
Gurda, David Allan Cates, Suzanne Swanson, Solveig Nilson, Lisa DuBois
Schmitz, Tatyana Krimgold, Kathryn Landseadel, Natalie Hinahara, Laura
Williams, Tegan Nia Swanson and the Bathtub Wine Collective. Thank you
to my ancestors, my aunties and my beloved parents Tom Healy and Gia
Interlandi for giving me life. And thank you to Marin, Silas and Anders for
(actually) everything.

Publisher: Leah Huete de Maines
Editor: Christen Kincaid
Cover Art: Natalie Hinahara
Author Photo: Anders Gurda
Cover Design: Elizabeth Maines McCleavy

Order online: www.finishinglinepress.com
also available on amazon.com

Author inquiries and mail orders:
Finishing Line Press
PO Box 1626
Georgetown, Kentucky 40324
USA

Contents

For Marin. And for me.

Bellyful

In our lineage a woman
heaved and loosed her child
into the arms of women

women holding her up,
offering

gifts of strength
          when hers is out
gifts of sweat
          when hers is spent

clothing her bellow in the hymns
of women. yes. sister. let. let. let.

Hair held by hands or hide
women showing her
as their mothers showed them

how to feed the tiny body
how to clean it, how to make offerings
to the gods and which gods

and which herbs stop the bleeding
andwhich meats she needs to eat
to be strong for the nights ahead

This is what a bellyful of love feels like,
they said.

Close time like an accordion—
          we all share one body

Stretch time like an accordion—
          we forget the purpose of the body

not a vehicle, not a temple, but a forest:
    food, shelter, medicine, shadow

or a storm on the cusp of its might

Upaya

I had seen your eyes in a dream, looking
up through folds of soft green cloth
wise eyes, knowing mine

In some late summer canyon I had heard
the quiet snuffle you made as I lifted you
from the birth water, held you to me

My job at the zendo was to shake
the heavy jute mats at dawn,
returning dust to desert

The hummingbird moth would
visit me then, lavender blossoms
whirling in its wing wake

Delight settled in my brain
made a place for you, an amygdala
print of feathered antennae

Now I come to this temple nightly
bearing full breasts, incense of sleep
to walk kinhin in noble silence

You are the hummingbird moth and I
am the lavender, as you latch and pull
I bow to your hunger, this dream

Mammals

The first full moon,
snowflake on her eyelash
animal, how I want to lick it off

nibble her ear
nuzzle her fuzz
fold her into my hide

leaving tracks and
traffic behind, we hunt
through a thicket of breath

What It Is, And Maybe Isn't

Before words come to limit you
            your mind is a hawk
                  your mind is a mirror
                        your mind is a myth of origins

What you know is wind
            through dry seed heads, bent
                  reeds, snow circles cast
                        on the burnt prairie

A marble of perfect knowingness
            growing slowly less luminous
                  evermore beautiful
                        as it becomes a living planet

Early April

My father told his teenage daughter
"there's nothing worse than being mediocre"
didn't mean it
but I metabolized the words
tried to excel
rather than to learn

Now I sit by a window
doing the worlds most ordinary thing
drinking tea—not well, not badly—
worshiping the averageness of her

Pudgy thighs, the long bones they cover,
ear whorls, tiny hips,
sturdy crop of honey-colored hair
two eyes, everybaby grey

Her heart beats the plain old way
lips yawn wide
if this is her greatest achievement
I'll be wreathed in pride

Alright Already

When her real parents come
will they find us like this?

I should start now:
wash the spit up from my neck
sanitize the bottle

pick up her pacifier and lick
the dusty surface clean

put on pants with my free hand

When her real parents come
will she look ready to go?

I'll find it now:
the little strawberry sweater
I always meant to put her in,

the matching cap
two socks

play some piano music with my free hand

Good thing her real parents
are coming, right?

I'll say "bring her by any time"
then close my eyes or
make plans with friends later

go back to wearing earrings
and drawing lists

neat check marks in
                empty boxes

Marvel: Us

The doors open for me at Target
because they know what I have done

I grew a body in my body,
made a person where there was none

How many women walk through life
with this triumph on their brow?

How many superheroes shop
for coffee in this aisle now?

My wound has not yet healed,
I'm still timid in my gait

But holy bloody hell
can you not see my fucking cape?

Count the hours of my labor,
the length of the tear,

the months of ill-fitting clothing
and enormous underwear

Add pushing out a baby
like any other clever ape

The hardest thing I've ever done
I did to earn this fucking cape

We cannot fly or shape-shift
or move things with our minds

Or keep our hungry children
from tantruming in line

Young mother hauling toddlers
a baby nestled in your nape,

I don't know much about you
but I see your fucking cape

Now fill your cart with diapers
vitamins and weeping

And a neon fucking sign that says,
"SHHH! BABY SLEEPING!"

I know the animal behind your eyes
searching for escape

But all that's left to do is rise,
let fly your blessed cape.

The Hundredth Hour

In my hundredth hour of rocking her to sleep
I tilt my head to the side, resting hers on my neck

Outside the window, a hawk mantles and flies
I am jealous of her lightness but not her freedom

This is not sacrifice: mine. yours. hurt. work. gift. owe.
All mean something different now that no one gives to get

In my hundredth hour of rocking her to sleep
I account for her vertebrae like a miser counting coin

I've never wanted anything so much as for her to stay
alive, gather her in like the last crop before rain

Tufts of breath on my collarbone, tiny weather
bringing a new season and anew

In my hundredth hour of rocking her to sleep
I wipe every third breath from the cold pane

A storm moves outside the window, thunder thrums
I hum to smooth over the first sharp slaps of rain

This gully-washer love, sending anything loose to the sea
except my tiny boulder, re-routing rivers

Requiem for Sleep
In haiku style

dawn, save your cheerful
grey light dove song mist rising
for someone who cares

…

because I can't sleep
I rub my soft belly
thinking of moss

…

tiny psychic knows
just when I push off from shore
lets her tempest fly

…

a spade lifting soil
does not consider the wish
of the nestled loam

…

an unshuffled deck
of apologies makes a
weird game of lost thought

…

lucky morning
horizon organizes
itself as words

…

neither sea nor sky
sleep is a poppy seed
in a madwoman's eye

Moro Reflex

She no longer
tries to fly
when falling

Maybe she trusts
my hands now
guiding her down

Maybe she has
forgotten the supple
sling of womb

Maybe her mind
is eroding instinct
to make itself modern

Soon she will
no longer
sleep in trees

Postpartum

You live in a house called mommy.
It controls the climate, gathers mail.

To birth a world you became Universe.
Now your power leaks out your breasts.

Bare bulbs flicker. You don't rest
within these walls of taking.

>   Touch your sternum and your face.
>   Find the window of your eye.

>   Broken glass, raided cache.
>   Countless heirlooms missing.

>   Dust collects in the caved corner
>   of your strangely vacant head.

When you scrawled "I can't do this"
on the wall, you didn't know:

Of all the broken things
your heart is the loudest

Broken like a dripping faucet,
inexhaustible.

>   Drip. Echo. Survive
>   the cracking of your mind.

>   Arrive in your spine.
>   Tall like the grass.

>   Find forgiveness rooted, leafing
>   a curious climbing vine.

You are Living in a Poem
Poem title from Naomi Shihab Nye

I. Germination

I love the way
she reaches for sunlight
seedling that she is
first taste of life
stretching her upward
and out

II. Laundry

If not put away
at least it is folded
like a plant out of place
full of flowers
if not evading chaos
at least making it lovely

III. Summer

The tomatoes
will never ripen
too much rain
we dance in it
her body
slippery
mouth busy
gumming
the drops

Name

after Kae Tempest

First it was a question
then it was a secret
now it changes a little
every time we speak it

how will it wander?
where will it settle?
your name, so tender yet
gaining grit and mettle

your name in the mouth of morning
your name on the breath of trust
your name on the ticket and boarding
and soaring away from us

the name your teachers call you
the name you use at work
the name the river gives you
in its language
of beavertail and birch

there's the name the ocean whispers
the first time you visit and the last
the name you live into
by learning from the past

your name in the mind of millions
your name fruiting on the farm
your name on the guest list
or tattooed on someone's arm

your name said in Gaelic
your name tracked in dust
you name remembered
then forgotten
then transformed
into something glorious

write it by the doorbell
write it on the tomb
I'll never forget
it written on the wall
in your delivery room

I can't follow where you go
but I'll tell you a thousand times
Mama is the truest name of mine
indelible, sealed, signed

I want to tell you
in way that makes you know
I love you no matter the name
you write in breath
on your window

Evening

after The Bath by Gary Snyder

In the tub
wreaths of steam
circle your fingers

Papa washes
your armpits, legpits
tiny vulva, feet

He remembers
Gary Snyder in the sauna
with his family
all warm and washing

naked and playful
smelling cedar, hot rocks
the slip of soap on skin

When I was pregnant
your papa wanted
to join our body, to feel
your stretch and squirm

his tether to you,
un-umbilical
is maybe stronger
for being chosen

Like Gary washing his
wife and son
sharing water, heat
one body moving in
tenderness
dark as the womb

strong as the braided beast
being born

July

I.

When the river is yellow
with great swirls of pollen
I remember she could die
Her presence so thick
a slow moving eddy
lazy with damselfly wings
samaras, summer gunk
She sucks the salt off my skin
leaves her teeth mark on my arm

II.

A Chicago driver
blew a stop sign
and dragged my friend's
toddler half a block

His mother held him
begging the empty air
maple leaves turning
no reason
red

III.

I know what I would do
if she died:
become a lava flow

burn and spit through
canyon and cut, Gila range,
North fork, Mogollon land

collect in the cliff dwellings
like flood trash, cool and harden
pack my wounds with ash
then rest my hand
in the print of the hand
of the woman

who built the wall
who outlived her own heart here
as women often do

IV.

Emmett Till soared
down a different river once
body stuck with samaras,
blood, foamed mud

Every mother tends
a hollow horror for him
for her, the one who waited
until she slipped beneath

the dark well of grief
and disbelief
and said "Let the people see
what they did to my boy."

I thread my heart on
her story line, we all do
Black and Brown mothers
wear it heavy across their chests

V.

Why would someone take your most perfect love and mutilate
its body?
Who would trench the flesh of an innocent thing?
I am harnessed to the questions, as I am to her.
Each a kind of haunting. Each a kind of prayer.

VI.

I kiss her eyelid twice
follow the willows home
our sweat combines
and becomes the river
thick with pollen
the river
leaves its teeth mark
on my arm

Fern

The egg
that made you

        grew inside me
        while I grew inside

                your grandmother

Uncountable
beginnings

        bubble within
        you

                bodies beloved

Fractal
we are

        each
        a chapter

                each a story of her own

Quitting, the Good Kind

Taty asked me how it would be
to live without striving
And I thought,
like birth

odd, as birth is labor, yes, pain, yes
work, the holiest
of work

I have seen her—the mother—
in the hours before
her mind knows
the baby
is coming

how her thighs swell, eyes quicken
face flushed wild, her body
bulges immense with
its own
knowing

I have held her hand, I have been
the hand squeezing another
I have heard the midwife
whisper beyond
words:

do not try to get the baby out. relax, and let the baby out.

So, what would it be like—she asks me
under a pencil diptych—
not to try?

it would be like birth

living as a body in a world of brains

urge. instinct. opening.

Arjuna and Krishna in the chariot
thundering toward a battle
no one sought
to win

it would be quitting the climb
and becoming the
mountain

it would be growing immense
with knowing that god
lives in my womb
and my only
assignment
is to

breathe and let her out

We

the pronoun
of parenthood

OUR first tooth
OUR bruised forehead
OUR swim lessons

I judge the mother
who has sunk herself
in her child

Until I arrive asking
if it's ok to bring
our coffee

into the store
we'd like to buy
a book, though she

cares for neither
besides the paper cup
or pages she will chew

later, I tell the cashier
we've pooped
and whose poop?

he doesn't ask
but maybe believes
we each filled our pants

acceptance is a bright sun
I squint into
ambling out the door

a bi-souled being
babbling to myself
in two tongues.

Mid-October

She eats a lady bug
What can you do?
Consider it food.

November

She walks
holding a block
in each hand

We all hold
conflicting truths
in tension

Or, in union

The nightly wreckage
and cherished dew
of her are

One braided length
of sweetgrass
and singe

One single
tentative step
to a waiting hand

This despair
does not erase joy
it is her midwife

We are not possible
without the torn, broken
I that made you

In our body
loss is the bass clef
wholeness is the treble

And I hear no conflict
in the chord

For Marin

I. Permission

It's ok to love
the obvious things
Moonshadow
Swallow flight
Thunder
So say the flies:
if your food is everywhere
you'll never be hungry

II. Blessing

It's ok to go blind
for a time
remember how to hear
first, to navigate
by touch
or by the time it takes
your heartbeat
to come back
from distant objects

III. Practice

It is ok to love
the difficult things
the car-killed crow
one wing rising
rhythmically from the road
a greeting for you, and
and the flies who
need no invitation

The bath, Sunday

Letting the water out a body sinks and
settles, washrag too, slack slump—does
she know she was once weightless?

I get you, rag. I absorb everything
the tears the blood the mud of my loves
fibers full of spilled juice and paintbrush water

this work has made me soft wide unbreakable

I stay where the water left me, getting heavy
heavy makes me slow, slow lets me be alone
alone is the only place I am sort of elegant

naked in the mirror I take my time
with the orange scented lotion, drawing
on unceded circles of skin—underankle

slope of neck, small hill of sacrum

I blow out the candle in my green-tiled temple
priestess of an odd sect, cult of life-givers
divine order of washrags, lifting
sinking in the tides of our lives

stopping the drain with our one wish

to drift
 a bit

longer

Kitt Healy is a mother, writer, facilitator and movement strategist for sustainable agriculture organizations. She is of Irish, German and Sicilian settler descent and currently lives on the present and ancestral lands of the Ho-Chunk people in Madison, WI. She has an MS in Agroecology from UW-Madison and a BA in Political and Social Thought from University of Virginia. When her hands are not writing, they are likely busy planting seeds, sprinkling herbs on something tasty, or wrangling her two rascally children.

www.ingramcontent.com/pod-product-compliance
Lightning Source LLC
Chambersburg PA
CBHW030052100426
42734CB00038B/1387